VALENTINES AND FORGERIES
MIRRORS AND DRAGONS

On the Cover:
Oil on Stone: Icon of St. George and the Dragon: XHR (by hand),
Evangelopoulos, Isle of Patmos, the Dodecanese, Greece

VALENTINES AND FORGERIES
MIRRORS AND DRAGONS

Poems
by
James McGrath

Illustrated by Catherine Ferguson

SANTA FE

© 2012 by James McGrath
All Rights Reserved.

No part of this book may be reproduced in any form or by any electronic or mechanical means including information storage and retrieval systems without permission in writing from the publisher, except by a reviewer who may quote brief passages in a review.

Sunstone books may be purchased for educational, business, or sales promotional use. For information please write: Special Markets Department, Sunstone Press, P.O. Box 2321, Santa Fe, New Mexico 87504-2321.

Book and Cover design › Vicki Ahl
Body typeface › Benguiat
Printed on acid-free paper
∞

Library of Congress Cataloging-in-Publication Data
McGrath, James, 1928-
 [Poems. Selections]
 Valentines and forgeries, mirrors and dragons : poems / by James McGrath ; illustrated by Catherine Ferguson.
   pages cm
   ISBN 978-0-86534-921-6 (softcover : alk. paper)
 I. Title.
 PS3613.C497V35 2012
 811'.6--dc23
                                                          2012041442

WWW.SUNSTONEPRESS.COM
SUNSTONE PRESS / POST OFFICE BOX 2321 / SANTA FE, NM 87504-2321 /USA
(505) 988-4418 / ORDERS ONLY (800) 243-5644 / FAX (505) 988-1025

DEDICATION

To my Dragon Year daughter Jeni Keleen
and to my Horse Year daughter Jain Kelain

TO MY DAUGHTERS

*Remember how the unblinking orange eyes
of your rabbit and monkey saw only what
was there in the darkness?*

When the world-dragon swirls the dust at your feet,
    hold tight to the stems of flowers.

If the wind of stolen words pains your ears,
    listen to the silence of the stones
    on the path you walk with ants and beetles.

Should the river-mirror rise over its banks,
    flooding the road into town, wait
    for the waters to settle, leaving mud
    for you to shape into a cup for tea.

When you venture into the field of knee-high grasses,
    let the greenness of their fingers tattoo
    the dreams of your future.

Should a dragonfly of forgery sew your lips together,
    know the thread is the first line of your poem
    that has no end.

When the night comes and there are no stars,
    remember the valentine story I sewed into
    your rabbit and monkey that began, "You are
    my daughters. The light I leave you is shining
    in your eyes . . .

        I love you,
            Your Dad

CONTENTS

ACKNOWLEDGEMENTS / 10
PREFACE / 11
INTRODUCTION by Ann Yeomans / 12

VALENTINES / 15

To Write is to Love Again 17
She Visits in the Night 18
Daisies. 19
This is What I Wanted. 20
Searching for a Reflection. 21
He Died Before I Could Hold Him . . 22
In Millie's Garden 24
How to Love 25
The Humming of Bees 26
The Bird With Folded Wings 27
Daniel 28
The Gift of Your Name 29
An Early Death. 30
It's How We Unwrap the Gift 31
Poem for Shama 32
This is How She Loved Me 33
The Real Thing. 34
Bird. 35
A Meeting in Yemen in a Time of Flood 36
Poem for Dana. 38
This is Where I See Your Face 39
What Poet Are You? 40
On Valentine's Day 41

FORGERIES / 43

Shadow Pen 45
Holly Berries 46
A Walk in the Jungle 47
The Forger 48
The Color of Ice Melting 49
Colors Lost in the Eyes of Artists . . 50
Drawing Dreams before Departing . 52
The Fish That Wished to Fly 53
I Pause a Moment 54
I Will Keep the Gate Open for You . 55
A Lawn Covered with Gravel 56
Leave-taking 58
The Poet's Autumn 60
Tiepolo's Ceiling 61
The Woman Who Lives Alone . . . 63
Writing in the Margins 65
Catching My Breath 66
There is a Fine Line 67

MIRRORS / 69

Who are You that I Write My Poems To? . . 71
Where Do Poems Live? 72
In the Time of Winter 73
When We Remove Our Sandals 74
Crumpling the Paper 76
Baptism 77
Self Portrait: January 2012 78
The Road 79
I Tell Myself How I Should Write a Poem . . 80
This is the Land Where I Live 82
The Genie 83
Feeding the Fire 84
Drawing with Crayons 85
Crickets 86

12 December 2008. 87
The Spaces Between Your Name and Mine . . 88
Self-portrait at 80 89
Poem for Laura Gilpin, Photographer 91
A Cup of Tea with Paulette 92
A Portrait of Uncle Nap. 93
Listening to Childhood Drawings 94
The Wind is Lonely 96
Breaking Camp 97
The Soft Edge of a Mountain 99

DRAGONS / 101

Time of the Dragon 103
Fragments 104
The Missing Parts 105
The Departure of William Witherup 106
Stealing Time 107
The Homeless Man 108
The Sound of an Echo 109
GUNS GUNS GUNS 110
MUST SELL HOME: Call 986-6066   112
The Loneliness of Ashes 113
My Winter Soldier 115
The Edge 116
The King at the Corner of Agua Fria
 and Guadalupe 117
Claws of a Lion 118
Shadows with Names 120
With Light on Water 122
Fishing with Brass Spinners 123
There are Hoodlums Inside Me 125
Ask Me for Bread and Water 126
The Last Icon 128

ABOUT THE COVER ART / 129
ABOUT THE ARTIST / 130
ABOUT THE POET / 131

ACKNOWLEDGMENTS

Quotations of John Burnside, Tony Hoagland,
Philip Levine, Charles Simic, Jorie Graham,
Nuala Ni Dhomhnaill, courtesy of Dennis O'Driscoll,
Quote Poet Unquote, Copper Canyon Press, 2008.
Manuscript preparation: Frances Hunter

PREFACE

I sat with Carl Jung this morning.
He said, "The task is to hold the opposites together,
the goal is not the heights but the center."

It is stimulating enough to be born in a Dragon hour on a Snake day in a Monkey month in a Dragon year, September 2, 1928, and now in my eighties, I have finally decided I am a paradox of valentines and forgeries, nights and days, mirrors and dragons, man and woman: bits and pieces of all those encounters I have had, from looking into the eyes of my ancestors to hoping my great-grandchildren will be true to themselves: wishes and dreams.

This collection, my fourth with Sunstone Press of Santa Fe, New Mexico, comes with contented clarity and confusion, being blessed with love-hearted friends and family and a healthy spirit for experiencing the world with a semblance of evolving wisdom and losses to be reincarnated.

These poems are gathered like the mixing of unplanted wild flowers and dandelion fluff. Perhaps I have shared nothing new except as the words love themselves and fill up the space where if we stand together we might hold hands to watch the sun rise once again.

—James McGrath

INTRODUCTION

In James McGrath you find a natural poet and a dreamer residing in a medial world who fluidly crosses between edges and borders. He has a genius for noticing boundaries and leaping beyond them, taking us with him. James had the wisdom to ask his friend Catherine Ferguson, retablo artist, to create evocative and imaginative drawings which provide an entry into the territory he is describing: a place of magic, fantasy, present/not-present, an as-if, make-believe place in the heart, an invitation to the world of the poet.

James trusted his intuition when the title of this book came to him, and he followed its lead. Each section seems to open a fictional space with a glance from a different angle towards what we consider reality. If you let yourself imagine . . .

A master at activating slumbering images, you'll notice his uncanny ability to take them by surprise and inhabit them. By becoming the images and dancing with the words, he experiences presences where others may see only outlines. His world is alive with beings we might not be able to see or be with were it not for his vision. Through animating and entering into the worlds he apprehends, our world is made richer.

There's nothing passive in James' work, as he gives life to what may seem to others to be lifeless. He doesn't write about things, but in response to, even in love with them. He may enter into other people's realities as if they were his own, with an ardent receptivity to that experience. He becomes an Iraqi woman, a wounded soldier, a homeless man.

What revealed itself to me in these poems is an understanding of the ephemeral energy between people, wildly bursting and transforming through longing. People inhabit and become enlivened by images in nature. Often violence is needed to break through and reach the words, the poem, the muse. Witness his extraordinary gift for synaesthesia: unlocking a mixture of sense to create the richest, juiciest brew of enjoyment, offering us the gifts and bouquets of his perception. While reading, I imagined being in his orchard, hearing the words like colorful apples on the trees, whispering birds, with glistening sun and gentle breeze: "The Real Thing."

Most eloquent to me in this volume is his openness to darkness, the trickster, to betrayal and loss, "the place I cut open my chest to give my heart to what loves me." There are echoes in James' writing of James Hillman's *Thought of the Heart:*

> *. . . psyche is the life of our aesthetic*
> *responses, that sense of*
> *taste in relation with things, that thrill or*
> *pain, disgust or*
> *expansion of breast, those primordial*
> *aesthetic reactions of*
> *the heart are soul itself speaking.*

In these covers, heart, soul and psyche are indeed speaking, if our hearts and ears are open.

Valentines and Forgeries, Mirrors and Dragons is a rich imaginal repast—may you be replete with the meal!

—Ann Yeomans
Archetypal Therapist
Santa Fe, New Mexico

VALENTINES

A naïve reader always assumes that a love poem is necessarily addressed to a person (either openly or in secret). Yet this is rarely the case, even when the poet says it is: it is love that the poet loves, not the seeming object of that love.
—John Burnside
La Traducriere, No. 17, 1999

To Write is to Love Again

When a poet writes of things hidden
        under stones or in dreams
        only nightmares leave behind,
        I implore them to plunge me deeper.

Sometimes a poet hints
        at the brownness of the horse.
        I want to inhale the sweat,
        to be stomped on by its hooves.

I want to be buried, memorialized
        in autumn leaves, then massaged away
        into a September orchard
        of ripe peaches being harassed by bees.

When a poet writes to the edge of the abyss,
        stops, turns around, waits,
        I want to be pushed over,
        to tumble and bounce against the stones,
        as I fall. If I do not reach the bottom
        in one piece, I can forgive the poet.
        I only want the terror of being torn open
        by a torrent of words.

I don't want a poet to boil me in a pot of stew
        leaving out the spices and the moment
        the heat is turned down forgetting
        the scorching and the burning.

I want my ears to be seared
        by the memory of abandoned love,
        my eyes to flame when I read
        of the emptiness that turns tears into steam.

And if I could write a poem like the stars fall,
        I would read to you tonight
        and be rekindled into a wildfire.

                                6 October 2006
                            Santa Fe, New Mexico

She Visits in the Night

She said I was in her dream last night,
    walked with her through tall grass
    to the river.

She said we sat on a fallen tree
    that stretched its arms
    across the rapids.

She said there were birds on the river
    and horses grazing in the field
    on the other side.

She said we whispered stories
    of barking dogs and the names
    of ladies in lace collars.

She said gray-blue voices
    of the wind were running
    from the clouds.

When she came to the part of the dream
    where I vanished, I began to cry.

I wanted her to brush the hair
    from my eyes.

I wanted her to reach into my pockets
    to pull out the poem
    I was hiding from God.

I never knew if her dream was real,
    if she was telling me what the river
    in her blood was speaking.

She visits in the night now
    when there is rain on the roof
    and the fire in the moonlight has died.

3 June 2008
Santa Fe, New Mexico

Daisies

When I see the night sky
      irrigated with daisies,
      I spiral my fingers apart,
      counting the petals,
      discovering if she still loves me.

This is the one secret
      I would never tell the moon.

25 February 2008
Galisteo, New Mexico

This is What I Wanted

I had no voice,
        yet I called out to open the door,
        to take it off the hinges,
        to spread out the carpet
        bleeding with faded flowers.

I had no hands,
        yet I reached out
        to catch the blood flowing,
        to catch it drop by drop,
        to wash my hands of the taste of vinegar.

I had no feet
        to run away from the crashing
        of glass breaking, silencing the moon
        rising over the mountain.

I wanted the snow to come early,
        to mound itself against the trees
        where our names were carved
        in foreign languages.

I wanted the sky to fall,
        to crush my skull,
        to make wind of the words
        I gave to you before I vanished.

I wanted you to know
        my arms were too weak
        to hold you any longer.

19 December 2007
Galisteo, New Mexico

Searching for a Reflection

This morning I see your figure in the phantoms
    left by a night bird that dreamed you.

You come and go,
    unexpected, uninvited.
    I don't invite ghosts
    when morning glories open their eyes.

When you arrive in a fog,
    I welcome your invisibility,
    even ask you to stay a while.

In all those years we dribbled time away,
    we never questioned the shape that time
    would leave behind.

For now, I only see you when your image
    floods the day in drought-driven light.

By noon, you will have vanished again,
    melted, turned into a hollow bird-bone flute.

If you come to me in a lost letter
    hidden in a pile of night leaves,
    I will twist and tumble about,
    vomiting those leaves into the air,
    calling them ravens.

I will speak to those ravens,
    telling them winter is coming,
    they must fly South to circle you
    with a crown of hibiscus.

I will tell them to watch for you
    searching a bottomless pool
    of sunset water, searching
    for your reflection for the last time.

                                3 November 2006
                                Galisteo, New Mexico

He Died Before I Could Hold Him

How many times did we say good-bye?

He enters my heart where all the silence
        is filled with his lonely wildness.

I hear his rippled laughter
        when he ran cold, shivering from the river.

He interrupts every song
        that summer colors leave behind
        in the morning garden.

There is no room for us
        in the bells of tulips.

He was all the music I needed to breathe.

I hear him snapping his brightness
        in the blazing fireplace.
        He leaves whispers in the ashes.

He colors every room
        in the memory-blue
        of holding hands
        between the pages of poetry.

If I sit long enough,
        the sounds that scuff across the floor
        vanish into fog that being too young
        sighs along the ground.

Now he arrives when the moon rises.
        He carries it in his arms
        when he knocks on my door.

How many times did we say good-bye?

There are questions that migrating birds
        ask when they are lost.

There are voices like mine
        that sit in trees
        just before the saw cuts them down.

7 February 2006
Santa Fe, New Mexico

In Millie's Garden
   —*in memory of Millie McGrath*

It is March, almost April.
It is always almost April.
I see you in your garden,
        your hands molding the expectant earth.

Your fingers flutter around green shoots
        of ferns and iris.

I see a red trowel in your hand.
        It shapes black dirt sculptures
        near the spears of tulips and daffodils.

You call the purple worms out of their sleep
        to make tunnels around bulbs and rhizomes.

I hear you humming *Alice Blue Gown*
        while scratching out chickweed
        and stray clumps of lawn grass.

There is a bed of lettuce
        and tomato plants on your mind.

As you move along your flower beds,
        spring comes and goes,
        summer heat calls for water just before dark,
        autumn hollyhocks stretch against
        the neighbor's fence.

You are the winter garden now
        that rests with stored shovels and rakes.

All the dirt under your fingernails
        that you saved over the years
        has been washed away.

And I have the warmth of memory
        to sow into my garden
        where I plant the seeds
        of your laughter and sighs.

                              5 March 2006
                              Santa Fe, New Mexico

How to Love

When the wind stops
        and the shadows cease to dance,
        I will ask a tree in my orchard
        to become my partner.

We will share the last apple
        before it falls.

20 October 2007
Santa Fe, New Mexico

The Humming of Bees

I want to be the door that opens
        from both sides or the window
        without a latch.

These are the ways into the house
        where I live.

Should you knock on my door,
        knock gently, but long;
        I may be sleeping.

If you wait to look into my window,
        choose a moon-filled night
        when the glass is a mirror.

It is a lonely bird
        that sees a winged stranger in the glass
        and flies into the window.

It is a messenger who rests
        on the doorstep when the sun
        plants a memory there
        when it snows.

Should you leave a message
        in the mailbox by the side
        of the road, sign it with the name
        a cloud has given you.

I will hear you humming like a thousand bees.

28 November 2008
Santa Fe, New Mexico

The Bird with Folded Wings

You are there woven into the rug,
>   the bird with folded wings,
>   the fallen flower petals.

I walk around you,
>   keeping dust from your eyes,

You are there under the table
>   in the corner, the shadow of chairs
>   hiding the splinters in your feet.

I sit hushed near your shoulders,
>   not touching, reading years
>   in the knots and grains of you.

Somewhere in the house are cupboards
>   of hand-painted dishes and cups
>   with chips and cracks where poems
>   have been caught whispering your name.

And in the woven quilt folded
>   at the foot of my bed,
>   I hear the click-clack of your needles
>   embroidering your days
>   into faded landscapes and autumn keepsakes.

Only now in the late years,
>   I ask the emptiness where you will go
>   when the stars have all fallen.

I touch your face, hold your hand,
>   smooth your hair.

Should someone pull up the carpet,
>   roll it into the corner, blinding you,
>   tying your wings to your body,
>   I will have enough words to free you.

I will have given the light in your eyes
>   to those who read as if the last poet
>   who ever wrote of your face had died.

>   *6 February 2010*
>   *Santa Fe, New Mexico*

Daniel
    for Daniel Forest

You say, there is one of you,
    a single man,
    breathing the air of mountains
    and pine trees, inviting stones
    and birds into your eyes.

I see the many men of you:
    the faces of you against my neck
    tasting the salt of me;
    the arms of you warming my
    shoulders, the many fingers of you writing
    indecipherable
    poems on my back and chest, lines
    of autumn-scented adjectives
    along my thighs, down my legs
    where the many toes of you fill
    the hollows behind my knees and
    make cross-hatches on my ankles.

It is the many men of you who close
    my eyes when you kiss me, who
    breathes the daily bread of your
    voice into my ears, who blushes
    my cheeks when you say, "I love you"
    in 24 languages between sunrise and
    sunset.

When I walk the road with the many men
    of you, I can not count the myriad
    sounds of your footsteps or the
    multitude of ways you pull clouds
    down from the sky when the sun
    blinds me.

I could never write the name of the
    many men of you. I would have to
    squeeze the red from poppies
    to create the indelible ink
    to stain the sky with DANIEL.

                                          28 November 2011
                                          Galisteo, New Mexico

The Gift of Your Name

You ask: What can I give you
        you do not already have?

If I told you, your gift would not
        be a surprise.

But let me leave a hint, a whisper,
        an echo against the cold stones.

Apple-blossom me,
        to fill my eyes with bursting seeds,
        my ears with words that burn holes
        in my poems.

Flower my winter
        with your forsythia brightness,
        to warm my breath with songs
        the house sparrow taught you.

Leave a brown bag
        of your sadness at my door
        in January so I can follow
        your footsteps in the snow
        before the sun melts them away
        and I never know your name.

30 December 2008
Santa Fe, New Mexico

An Early Death

Whispering to you
      is arranging flowers
      in your hair:
      one single breath
      holding falling leaves
      between apple branches
      and stones.

This is where we danced,
      caressed by bees
      gathering honey
      for winter hives.

My silence with you now
      is the mountain
      I climb when the moon
      fails to appear in your eyes.

My silence is one single breath
      steaming the window in my heart,
      where I write "I Love You"
      with my glass fingertips.

This is where
      we left one another:
      you following shadows
      of geese flying South,
      me staying behind,
      carving your name
      in the bark of the night.

23 October 2008
Santa Fe, New Mexico

It's How We Unwrap the Gift
—for Paulette Frankl, dreamer-artist

It's how we unwrap the gift,
        the morning light that presses
        against our door and taps on the window.

No need for skillful fingers
        to open the knots, pull the bow,
        unwind the night, free the stars
        and sounds on the ceiling.

How do we interpret the wrappings,
        the cellophane and tissues,
        the silk ribbons, the veins of string
        connecting what is never asked for:
        the moonlight, the wind on water, the scent of sage?

In a pot of February daffodils
        are buds waiting to unfold.

If we could become a bud for a time,
        to unfold, to give color to a room,
        we would be so still, expecting nothing
        in return, not even to know
        if there are eyes watching us.

It is only on a sheet of white paper
        we can write "Thank you."
        as the earth says "Thank you"
        to the sun and the snow.

6 February 2010
Santa Fe, New Mexico

Poem for Shama
—for Shama Beach, poet-friend

She sits in the sun,
        bare feet in the Spring plume of grass,
        crickets chirping,
        her hair calling clouds into her garden.

She is of the earth,
        holds purple petunias softly on her doorstep,
        lilacs beginning to scent
        her neighborhood with memories of her twins.

She sits in the sun,
        presses her pen on the pages
        of her unlined notebook
        to write of a life of moons and moths.

She has a cat the color of melting chocolate
        that lies softly on her bed
        when she dreams of New York
        or morning croissants in Paris.

This is a lady of the earth
        where a candle by her bedside
        gives a light to inscribe the images
        in a poem on her ceiling.

She spends her days among the footprints
        of abandoned lovers
        who made mandalas of rainbows
        between her book covers.

This is a woman who tells stories
        that spellbind children
        and brings voices into their gardens.

She sits in the sun, even at night,
        when stars fall into her heart,
        giving her the gift of eternal youth.

7 May 2007
A Happy Birthday to Shama Beach
Santa Fe, New Mexico

This is How She Loved Me

She said if you climb to the top
       of the mountain, you can put
       a bit of cloud in your pocket.

She said watch the bamboo bend
       under the snow. There is strength
       in being yielding.

She said write your name in water.
       All truth flows to the sea.

I saw her standing at the edge of night.
       She held a red poppy.
       She smelled of lilac.

I watched her open a book of poems.
       Radiance held the pages open.
       Her eyes never closed.

I remember how her hand held the air,
       a cup of freshly-squeezed Spring.

I remember how the flowers in her garden
       filled the spaces between
       when she was young and her old age.

Now when memory tells the story
       of how she loved me, I know
       the earth is her breathing
       under the wings of butterflies.

Now when I despair, I can walk my road
       between the lines of two fences
       and feel at home.

I don't need to know where I am going
       to be there.

18 May 2007
Santa Fe, New Mexico

The Real Thing

There is that open space
    between the trees in my orchard,
    where grass is short,
    the boughs low,
    the sky drops around me when I hold my arms open.

This is where the path spreads out,
    one side wild plum,
    three sides apple.

This is where people have gathered
    to read poems, to celebrate
    birthdays, weddings,
    to share foods, fruits,
    to embrace one another.

This is where one hundred women
    could lie face down together,
    becoming mothers of earth again,
    where one hundred men
    could sit back-to-back together,
    feeling one another's spine,
    sharing the softness of their bodies again.

This is a sacred place, where I walk in circles,
    humming like a bee calling out my name,
    speaking with ancestors
    on my tongue,
    listening to the silence that can never be filled.

This is where the wind is breathing,
    asking for nothing,
    where the earth waits
    to be loved over and over again.

5 February 2009
Santa Fe, New Mexico
Published in New Mexico Poetry Review, Spring 2010

Bird
   —for John and Kate McGrath

I am learning a new language
>that has no words I recognize.

It begins in morning light
>before the sun hums gold syllables
>into tree branches.

This is the bouncing-brown speckled
>language of small birds
>with big family names: sparrow, finch,
>towhee.

This is a language that describes
>what night has left behind,
>that fills the garden with a dance
>of flittering feathered light.

There are no words sprouting from the earth,
>only a rococo crossword puzzle
>of flutters and flurries that give clues
>to where the world begins.

This is catching the ripples on water
>when the wind touches it, when light
>searches for a place to rest,
>when the first and last word may be bird.

8 April 2009
Galisteo, New Mexico
Published in New Mexico Poetry Review, 2010

A Meeting in Yemen in a Time of Flood

We stood together alone on the bridge into town,
    only because she had fallen against me
    when the wall of water hit the bridge we were standing on.

She clung to my shoulders in the sweep of water
    swirling down the river bed at the West Gate
    to the Old City.

Her burkha was entangled, twisted about us,
    her scarf and veil torn from her head,
    her stream of hair the color of mud.

The kohl about her eyes ran in black rivulets
    down her cheeks.

She was shaking. I was shaking.

min faDlak, law samaHt.

Excuse me, please. *min faDlak, law samaHt.*

That was all we could shiver in conversation,

I could tell from her face, her eyes wide, sad,
    crying, that she was apologizing for the river,
    the water, the mud, our entanglement, our debris.

We stood there in the hot sun, in the whispering
    flood waters.

In the corner of her burkha she had tied a flat loaf
    of bread. Miraculously, she unwrapped the bread
    with her pomegranate-tattooed fingers.

She fed me a bit of crust. It had a pocket
        of Taiz honey that burst and ran down my chin.

She laughed, fingered off the honey, offered
        her sweetened fingertips to my tongue.

I laughed. Mud was drying on our legs and arms.
        The water receded with sweet bread crumbs
        floating to the south where the river ran away
        with our secret.

                                          January 1993
                                          Sana a, Yemen

Poem for Dana
—*for Dana Negev, poet-friend*

She sat beneath the plum blossoms,
    opened her flower sunrise fan.
    Butterflies appeared, singeing
    her fingers with blue flames.

Plum blossoms fell into her eyes:
    morning stars.

Her wrist was a violin bow
    opening and closing the flowers,
    her face a peony.

In the mystery, a street musician
    hummed with bees:
    midday songs.

At twilight, the breathing of her fan
    gave wings to her hair:
    doves listened.

In the darkness, more blossoms fell,
    becoming fireflies. They gave light
    to her poems burning through the night.

At dawn, the flowers on her fan wilted.

She sits alone, painting blossoms
    of plum on her breasts.

18 November 2008
Santa Fe, New Mexico

This is Where I See Your Face

This is where I see your face.

There where the watercolors have run together,
      coloring your tears the green
      of a jealous mountain.

There where the dartings under water
      are silver-eyed trout.

There in the center of a tulip
      where a bee has suffocated in sweet pollen.

There at the edge of the sea, where clumps of foam
      have written your name in the sand.

There where the wind has crinkled clouds
      in a bottomless lake, reflecting
      the shape of your heart.

There in the silence of a mirror,
      where candlelight has died of neglect.

There in fire, where your letters of passion
      have left ashes for the gods.

This is where I see your face next to mine.

10 September 2009
Santa Fe, New Mexico

What Poet Are You?

I looked into one book after another,
      searching for the flower
      pressed against her heart.

I had forgotten if it was a full-faced blue pansy
      or petals from a rose
      placed between two pages
      in a book of white paper tears:
      her sign that it was something living.

Now I am fumbling with my books of poems,
      looking for the remnants of her memories.

Emily Dickinson does not have it,
      nor Neruda.

Rilke could be holding it loosely
      among his letters to a young poet.

I was young when I first saw the flower.
      Mary Oliver was on the shelf, about to be opened
      by my own dammed-up thesaurus.

I can feel the hot embers
      of the faded colors on my bookshelf.

Perhaps a cup of tea will help just now.

Perhaps I will remember what poet is holding her garden voice,
      waiting to brush the scent of her words against my cheek.

                              4 November 2006
                              Santa Fe, New Mexico

On Valentine's Day

How cautious we are, giving our Valentine in secret,
coding our names into:
      "Guess who."
      "Your secret Valentine."

How cautious we are,
      holding our children at arms' length.
      They reach out,
      their eyes speaking:
      "Hug me."
      "Hug me."

We shape the sweetness of cookies
      into heart shapes,
      the shape that we learned early
      was the shape of a heart,
      forgetting the rhythm of heart beats
      when saddened or threatened.

What is the shape of your heart?
      Doctors know.
      It's in a book.

There is another heart shape
      in a poem.
      It is the sound of your name,
      the imprint of your hand
      on my shoulder,
      from the morning we first met,
      the shape of the space you left behind
      when you went away.

13 February 2006
Santa Fe, New Mexico

FORGERIES

*The making of poems is mysteriously
tied up with not-knowing, with
willing ignorance and an openness
to mutation.*
   —Tony Hoagland
   The American Literary Review
   July – August 2003

*To me it's always open house;
If you want it and it doesn't exist,
just make it up.*
   —Philip Levine
   So Ask
   2002

Shadow Pen

There is an itch in my pen
        that holds back lies and truths.

Even if I hold it firmly,
        squeeze its point into the paper,
        it tells only a part of the story.

Perhaps the story is too green,
        no blooms in the branching sentences,
        no budding phrases.

First words begin with capital letters
        to make them important,
        first kisses,
        first deaths,
        each with a capital letter.

This pen—the child of the hand—
        speaks when spoken to.
        It will never say everything,
        even if it were to be left alone
        on the last sheet of paper in the world.

20 October 2006
Albuquerque, New Mexico

Holly Berries

> "I tell myself I am not looking for God"
> —Richard Rodriquez,
> Best American Essays, 2009

I found God before I knew his name.

I carried a round white stone in my pocket
    on my walk to Sunday school.

Along the way, the camellia bushes were vibrating
    with bird song. Too many bouncing sparrows to count.

I wanted to smell the long, yellow twisted hair
    of Jesus in the classroom.

I want to invite Him home to dinner for salmon
    and potatoes.

I wanted to slip the white robe from his shoulders.
    Did he have chest hair like my dad?

The cracks in the sidewalk had shoots of new
    green grass near Prospect Street.

Streetcar tracks on 54th Street were silver lines
    of a long distance poem I could walk humming,
    "Jesus loves me, this I know." I thought this was
    a love song.

There were red berries on the big holly tree
    in the front yard.

I wanted to eat them.

4 December 2011
Santa Fe, New Mexico

A Walk in the Jungle

When I left the museum,
    I continued drawing, counting
    the black birds in the wheat field.

They erupted from the frame, plucking out my eyes
    until everywhere there was blackness
    and the scalding heat
    of "You're not good enough!"

When I left the lecture room,
    I continued writing, pouring
    line after line of watery adjectives
    on the burning fire.

The words burned holes in the arms
    of my winter coat
    until, armless, I called
    for a wheelchair and a large pink eraser.

But those days were before
    the apricot blossoms
    made light-filled pools
    on my table.

Now when I hold a raindrop
    up to my lips, I can taste
    the beginnings of conversations
    between the mountain and the moon.

It was only when I knew my name
    was not my name
    that I could speak into the ears of tigers.

23 March 2007
Santa Fe, New Mexico

The Forger

He was the moon rising
        over the Sangre de Cristo Mountains.

He never sat silent
        when it rained.

He was the icicle melting
        from the eaves in winter.

His hands held the heat of sunrise
        before the birds burst from frozen ground.

His eyes were the gun-sights
        on his hunting rifles.

His scent was the vapor
        of boiling desert herbs.

I loved him when he ruffled the feathers
        of magpies, changing broken twigs into poems.

I loved him when he spoke my name
        with his breath on my winter shoulders.

I loved him when he sprouted seeds
        in the palms of his hands.

He is the shadow forging my name
        to blank sheets of paper.

27 November 2009
Santa Fe, New Mexico

The Color of Ice Melting

I envisage all the words, colors, faces,
        hands at the tip-of-my tongue.

If I gather the words together
        to shape a phrase, a description,
        a picture blazes
        of where we danced among noon-hot sage,
        stirred up dust.

        I would have few words.
        The sounds would be Spring and Rain.

If you would press your hand to the small of my back
        I would recoil in bliss,
        melt my shoulders into your breasts,
        sweat sweet dreams on your pillow.

        I would have few words.
        The colors would be Bougainvillea and Guitars.

If I could mold your profile into clay,
        turning you to face the mountain one day,
        then to face the West,
        where the sun melts the desert into lakes of lava,
        you would see why I stare at you
        in the night, where the colors are stars.

What lies at the tip-of-my-tongue
        is what I love most,
        what bites my lips,
        what I feed on.

        It is the years I have been nourished
        by your touching me in the silence.

What words are left are indecipherable
        as the voices of the tides
        going out over small stones
        turning them on their backs.

The sound and color would be Ice Melting.

11 March 2006
Santa Fe, New Mexico
Published in Oracle, Volume 6, 2007

Colors Lost in the Eyes of Artists
—for Catherine Ferguson

Across the floor
>scattered tubes from the paint box
>melt into pristine pine boards.

Alizarin Crimson, the sunset lips
>of my first love, the smear
>of a burn from pinching the candle
>before I sleep.

Naples Yellow, the darkening sulphur
>from the pit near Pompeii,
>a bruised pear in a still-life
>of Caravaggio.

Cobalt Blue, a swish of John Marin's
>Main Coast before the storm strikes
>Cranberry Island, before the last
>lobsterman secures his boat.

Viridian Green, the rotating orbs
>of Kandinsky when Spring blinded him,
>crushing his skull with the first leaves
>of the Volga elms.

Ivory White, the see-through mist
>of Rembrandt's papers:
>not quite narcissus white,
>not quite rising-moon white.

Mars Black, the edges of cows and chickens
>in Chagall's farmyard. He wants them
>linear and moving. A cow is a cow
>even when it floats above a red barn.

Cerulean Blue, a Matisse chair in sunlight,
> the sun bleeding through windows
> where his shadow sits alone
> in a yellow chair.

Gamboge Yellow, poisonous enough,
> edgy enough to demand an ear
> to be cut off before the postman comes
> to collect the mail, sharp-toothed
> as the dog.

Raw Umber, Cadmium Orange, blessed in Tahiti
> by Gauguin. Even today the palm trees press
> phantoms over beaches where bones
> of the painter's memory lie alone
> in honey-clustered drift.

Payne's Gray, the scabrous flesh
> of Grunewald's Christ in Colmar.
> The stench has colored the walls
> and discolored the carpets.

The artist stands in awe
> of what lies breathing on the floor.
> When she falls on her knees in prayer,
> she will never squeeze her paint tubes
> to emptiness.

> > > 8 February 2008
> > > Galisteo, New Mexico

Drawing Dreams Before Departing

I look out the window
      with my pen and paper.

I draw a peach tree
      but the buds keep bursting open
      and the birds are scattering seeds
      from the wooden feeder.

I can not draw fast enough.

The buds turn pink.

I must get my watercolors prepared.

The birds have flown away,
      lined nests with grama grass
      and horsehair from the barbed wire.

Peaches have formed.

Watercolors are dried.

Visitors have arrived and left.
      They stole the peaches.

I never pull the curtains
      across the window.

I must watch the peach tree
      and the birds that empty
      the feeder before I go blind.

I know this:
      it is the glass that keeps me
      from becoming the bark on the tree,
      that keeps me from flying with the birds.

                              30 March 2008
                            Galisteo, New Mexico

The Fish That Wished to Fly

He could not explain why
      the red-hot coals
      could burn my fingers.

When I picked them out of the ashes,
      they would stare and blink
      like words in a poem
      I did not understand
      that left fire in my eyes.

Once he read a story to me
      about a fish that wished to fly.

That night I dreamed,
      my body had watery eyes
      and glittering fins.

I flew to the top of the mountain.

He was there singing to silent birds.

When I awoke, my room was filled with feathers.

28 November 2008
Santa Fe, New Mexico

I Pause a Moment

Friend, I want to tell you
        what I most remember of you
        being in the world with me.

I pause a moment,
        see you walking across a dune,
        your footprints filling with sand,
        your shadow always just out of reach.

You were the one I wanted to follow.

Now you are running out of the river,
        more than wet. You are the river god.
        Your name is water.

Now you are reading. All about you are books,
        their titles hidden. The air is filled
        with fire and smoke. You are burning
        from too many things to do.
        I am sitting in the corner,
        watching the room blaze and char.

Now you are sleeping, your body floating,
        hovering near the ceiling over our bed.
        You are tapping on the plaster,
        seeking a place to fly through.

You left me behind years ago.

I have stopped waiting for your postcards.

Friend, I'll know when you have reached
        the place you are seeking. There will be
        a white sheet of paper in my mailbox
        with your tenderness pressed into its silence.

                                    6 August 2006
                                Santa Fe, New Mexico

I Will Keep the Gate Open for You

You said you would return.

We have waited here beside the garden,
> the birds and I.

You said you would bring flowers.

Even now in Spring, hollyhocks and columbine
> wait for you, keep their buds in anticipation.

You said you would float your shadow behind you.

With the sun in a cloudless sky,
> your shadow would be the map to my heart.

You said your shoes were wearing thin,
> your clothes had holes.

I will have needle and thread for you.
> I will have leather sandals for your feet
> and patches of denim for your jeans and shirts.

You said you had lost the watch
> your father gave to you.

This land is timeless. The birds sing
> the time of day. The stars describe
> the time of night.

You say you are sad and sit on a stone
> in loneliness.

The hillside behind the home here
> is sculptured with stones
> waiting for your arrival.

I will keep the gate open for you.

Birds and I are waiting in the rosebushes.

A magpie has the house-key in its mouth.

17 April 2008
Santa Fe, New Mexico

A Lawn Covered with Gravel

She went to the flower shop
        every morning at 7 o'clock.

She unlocked the doors, sprayed the orchids,
        pinched the faded and dead gladiolus
        blooms from their stalks,
        smiled at the African violets.

She gave fresh water to the roses
        in the coolers, changed the maidenhair
        ferns in the iris bouquets, checked
        for brown spots on the gardenia corsages.

She snipped limp leaves from
        the hanging baskets of petunias.

She was a floral assistant
        well into her nineties.

When her legs ached after her lunch hour
        and there was a tightness in her thumbs,
        she decided to retire.

They gave her the choice of flowers
        for the next six months,
        to be delivered every Friday.

At the end of six months,
        her fingers became inflamed.
        Her hand looked like plant cutters.

She could hardly butter her toast.

She had dreams of the moon,
        spotted brown like old gardenias.

Her camellia bush lost its buds.

Her south garden chrysanthemums
        lost their petals and became
        infested with small gray slugs.

She closed her windows, ordered
        a bouquet of plastic roses,
        gave her vases to the Salvation Army
        thrift store in South Tacoma.

She stopped bathing with scented soaps,
        changed her flowered sheets for
        plain white poplin.

She let grasses fill her bed of iris.

She covered her lawn with gravel.

12 August 2007
Santa Fe, New Mexico

Leave-taking

Before I leave
      I want to stand naked,
      hidden inside my skin,
      next to the model
      in Michelangelo's studio.

I want to hear the fall of marble chips
      on the floor.

I want to feel the sculptor's eyes
      caressing the neck of the model,
      to feel his fingers molding
      the chest and the genitals.

I want to stand naked
      next to that model,
      to taste the heat
      in the strength of shoulders,
      the firmness of flesh in stone.

I want to see tears from the sculptor's
      eyes become the sparks from his chisel.

Is there silence between the hammer
      and the chisel, or is there
      an angel singing in the blossoms
      outside the studio window?

Does the floor tilt toward
      where I sit with the model?

Will we roll together into the sculptor's arms
      when the figure is finished?

There is no breathing of dust
        in this studio.

There is only the sound of breath
        from the piercing arrows
        of the sculptor's eyes
        as he carves away the excess stone
        to free what he loves.

And when it is over and he leaves
        his studio, I will dress the model
        in my clothes, gather the fallen chips
        from the floor to eat them
        as my heart eats the days
        I have left to live.

30 March 2009
Galisteo, New Mexico

The Poet's Autumn

He must respond to
>a slight cut from the razor
>of a crow's wing,
>a picking of the scab from a death
>held open by guilt,
>autumn leaves that open the veins
>where memories of bruised knees
>are taped with band-aids and saliva.

He can never rake enough autumn leaves.

If the fire sends sparks into his eyes,
>he might blink, pull back to wait
>for the flames to burn down
>so he can read the ashes
>without burning his tongue.

What he responds to is the book
>of blank pages, his hand poised.

If he lets his shadow pass without
>naming it, he might lose his life.

His late years are not for gathering
>the leaves into piles. The best is
>to gently hold each leaf, follow
>the arteries from one side
>to the other side. Here is the map
>of his journey.

There is no blood in autumn leaves.

The trees stand still, naked.

He will stand there with them,
>waiting for the sky to paint him blue,
>waiting for the last leaf to fall,
>pressing the image of what he loves
>into his skull.

17 November 2008
Santa Fe, New Mexico

Tiepolo's Ceiling
   —*for Jennifer Carrasco, artist-friend*

Tiepolo had sad dreams of Icarus
        when he was four.

He thought his pillow was a cloud.

He thought his mother's billowing apron
        a cloud, his father's pantaloons clouds.

At five, Tiepolo saved jars of soapy water;
        he would shake them, making clouds
        for his aunts and uncles.

His school-friends thought him crazy.

At six, he was the first to waken
        to climb onto the roof,
        to drink the clouds.

He was intoxicated with clouds at seven.

By the time he was eight, he told his tutors
        his name was Cumulus, signed his letters
        Cumulus.

His father was not happy with his change of name.

One Friday at the age of ten, he locked
        the door to his room, painted his ceiling
        with pink, white, orange clouds,
        made a self-portrait peering out
        of a blue-eyed sky.

His father was bewildered.

It was only when Tiepolo painted the ceiling
        of the Church of the Gesuati in Venice,
        a cosmos of clouds, angels, cherubs,
        blue-eyed sky did his father rejoice in
        his reaching for heaven.

Today, the clouds over the Sangre de Cristo
        Mountains flow East all summer.

They come to Venice to join the angels
        and cherubs.

Tonight when Tiepolo floats across the ceiling
        of my room, I will dream I am a cloud.

8 August 2008
Galisteo, New Mexico

The Woman Who Lives Alone

She speaks of aging:
>the morning pains,
>the wakefulness when the moon
>breaks the glass in her window.

She will not answer her telephone
>when it rings. The caller might be
>someone who loves her.

She goes to the post office early in the day,
>in case there is bad news.
>She will have the entire day to worry.

At noon, she has a choice of a lunch
>she would enjoy, like a BLT, or something
>healthy, like a garden salad.
>She chooses the salad with olive oil
>and vinegar dressing. No coffee.

She thinks about her Will,
>goes to the file on Sundays to be certain
>her children are still listed as sole beneficiaries.

She never goes to church any more. She doesn't
>believe God cares about her. It was the doctor
>who cured the cancer.

In the afternoon, she tries to nap, to rest her heart,
>to ease the pain in her legs, to put her feet up,
>out of her shoes.

At dinner, she talks to her cats. They sit
>and listen to her stories of a happy marriage,
>to her anxiety if she should visit her daughter
>who married an alcoholic and cries a lot.

Before bedtime, she imagines she might not wake up.
>Should she ask her neighbor to call her at 7:30,
>just in case?

In her dreams, she speaks with angels. They have
soothing musical voices. They tell her
they love her. They look like the girl
in the photograph on her night-stand.

12 June 2007
Santa Fe, New Mexico

Writing in the Margins
—for Annie Osburn, who writes in the margins

In elementary school, he etched his initials
        into his desk near the glass ink-well,
        rubbed black ink into the letters,
        making his J M like two cracks in the wood.

His teacher never caught him.

In high school, he wrote his name in adhesive tape
        on the back of his green raincoat. Strangers
        called out to him from street corners.

His parents never said a word.

In college, he wrote poems to the girls
        in Kamola Hall, called them Sweetie and Cute.
        He never signed his name.

His roommate called him crazy, said girls don't like poems.

When the divorce lawyer wanted him to sign
        final papers, he wrapped his hands in bandages,
        said he could not write his name.

He took a plane to Paris.

Now that he is older with a fringe of gray hair,
        wearing glasses when he reads or writes,
        he puts an X at the end of his poems
        where his name should be.

His readers never know the difference.

His poems are moist with fog, and a mist
        covers his paper, like the haze that stones
        breathe in when the river floods in winter.

                      17 November 2009
                      Galisteo, New Mexico

X

Catching My Breath

I will call out to the fire
        breathing in the corner.

I will ask it not to leave ashes behind
        in the shape of my father sleeping.

I want it to burn fingerprints from the glass.

I will ask it to purse its winter-red lips
        into the handle of a pair of scissors
        to cut the ribbons holding footprints
        in the snow.

I will call out to the stranger across
        the road to keep the gate open,
        to read WELCOME in four languages
        that I write at my doorstep.

I will ask the birds flying South
        to carry the mountain on their backs,
        to bring songs of wandering poets
        to the orchard when they return next Spring.

13 November 2009
Galisteo, New Mexico

There is a Fine Line

What is there between water and ice,
        ice and water?

How to fill the space between heart and soul,
        birdcage and branch?

On the open field between four fences,
        the world spends its gifts, unwrapped,
        without a single knotted ribbon. This
        is the place to leave questions under stones.

Libraries are for filling vacancies
        left by loved ones.

Long walls of empty frames
        are for self-portraits to be painted
        in faded tones of childhood blue
        and the peppermint stripes of war-torn flags.

What is there between fire and ashes,
        ashes and fire?

How to fill in the space between what
        I whispered to you and what you heard?

Stones in the wall are carved
        with faces that never close their eyes.

I name them Father and Mother and Beloved.

The day that I add another layer of stones
        to the wall, I will smooth them, rubbing
        the palms of my hands, erasing the years
        in the lines between my fingertips and my heart.

12 April 2010
Galisteo, New Mexico

MIRRORS

*Poems are other people's snapshots
in which we recognize ourselves.*
—Charles Simic
The Unemployed Fortune Teller
1991

Who are You that I Write My Poems To?

When you reach out to take my hand,
       it is filled.
       I hold my inspired poem-pen
       firmly between fingers.

I have no name for you.

You bring me the crackle of sparks
       when my feet stir up the summer dust
       along my road.

You are the image created by migrating birds.

You are the lover I could tell no one about.

You are the stranger on the train to Paris,
       the poet who read at Keane's Pub,
       the cat that died too early,
       the bird-watcher, the shadow in Shibam,
       the thief, the tortured soldier, the rapist,
       the oracular voices in the orchard.

You look over my shoulder while I write
       my poems to become words on paper:
       the words that press my back into spaces
       I can not fill, the words that give heat
       to my eyes, burning holes in the air
       so I can breathe.

I write "I love you" in blood in my dreams.

You are the eyewitness I leave in the mirror
       when I turn out the lights:
       the effigy I carve on the basalt stones
       of the mountain.
       You will be decipherable one day
       in the far future by saints and mystics,
       who have been reincarnated
       as butterflies and dragons.

                                   4 March 2006
                               Santa Fe, New Mexico

Where Do Poems Live?
—*for Marcia Starck, poet-friend*

They dwell in tree branches behind me,
      calling like red-winged blackbirds
      in the wild rosebushes.

They lodge here under my feet in loose stones,
      twisting into obscure phrases
      echoing the thunder from over the hill.

They clump together in light-filled piles
      of winter leaves, fingers of grass
      pushing up between them.

They inhabit the buds on the gooseberry bush
      and the blushing twigs of wild plum.

These are the hints of poems
      that this sun-ripened day of March
      has given to me.

But the day is too fresh
      to gather verbs and adjectives
      for the nouns of the day.

These are the beginning of Spring
      behind my back and under my feet.

The Winter was long and dark.

I need the shudder of the thunder
      and those buds of wild plum to burst open
      before a poem about blue skies
      and songbirds takes flight.

9 March 2007
Santa Fe, New Mexico

In the Time of Winter

I wrap the time of Winter around my shoulders,
      tie the time of Winter about my feet.

Along the road there is snow to walk in
      and ice to carve
      into chunks of Spring.

A flock of sooty crows
      carouse in the junipers,
      spreading their voices to melt the ice.

There are tracks of rabbits, leading
      to where poems lie waiting for the moon
      to rise over the mountain.

Somewhere near the river the steam of
      warming horses form cloud-maps for
      migrating geese to rest on sky-filled pools.

There is no place to hide on Winter mornings.

Even snowflakes have huddled together,
      waiting for children to become angels
      on their breasts.

I wrap the time of Winter around my shoulders,
      where the ghosts of Winters' past
      are pressing me into prayer.

I tie the time of Winter about my feet
      to walk where light has burned
      holes into the darkness.

22 January 2009
Santa Fe, New Mexico

When We Remove Our Sandals
—for Ann Yeomans, dear friend of dreams

> And in its midst he sowed small worlds in my image
> and likeness;
> steeds of stone with manes erect
> and amphorae serene
> and the slanting backs of dolphins
> Ios   Sikinos   Seriphos   Mylos
> —Odysseus Elytis, from *Axion Esti, Genesis III*

Ios speaks:
> I have spoken with dolphins.
> They speak of leaving the sea to jump after songs
> circling the earth from the lyres and flutes of goddesses.
>
> They speak of following the shadows of seabirds,
> beseeching them to be carried to their nest,
> to be feathered, to fly.

Sikinos speaks:
> I have spoken with cicadae in the heat of summer,
> when lemons burst their skins from too much sun.
> Their acids stain my cloak, turn my silver bracelets
> into gold-eyed moths that shine, holding darkness
> in their wings.

Seriphos speaks:
> I have spoken with water in the days of drought.
> We have gambled the seeds of asphodel and the roots
> of Delphic olive trees.
> Should water lose the game to me,
> I would not take the prize: the oracle in you would die
> of thirst. All my amphorae have been emptied.

Mylos speaks:
    I have spoken with trees.
    In their stillness, I must tie my ears
    to their lowest limbs, where humans and silent horses
    wait in deep shade. It is in this place that the tree
    separates the cries of humans from the laughter of gods.
    These are the poems I will leave behind when I die.

The four friends, Ios, Sikinos, Seriphos and Mylos,
    have left the city. They walk behind us
    when we remove our sandals to walk barefoot, listening to
    stones and pine-needles.

9 July 2009
Santa Fe, New Mexico
After Elytis

Crumpling the Paper

The poet could have said No,
        could have put the pen down,
        crumpled the paper,
        got up from the chair,
        made a cup of tea.

The poet could have said No.
        Instead, she gripped her pen firmly,
        squeezed love and hate in swirls
        across the paper.

She made scars of beauty and shadow.

She made blood run from moon and stars.

She thought the ghosts lying on the floor
        at her feet were patterns in the carpet.
        When they touched her cheek,
        their tongues tasting her tears,
        she dug her pen more deeply.

Now, when she reads her poems in public,
        ravens stop talking,
        mirrors lose their faces,
        old men add rose petals to their names.

4 November 2009
Santa Fe, New Mexico
Published in New Mexico Poetry Review, Spring 2010

Baptism
—for my poet friend Cynthia West

This May morning, the green tips of the willows
        near the river pointed at one another,
        daring to open.

Were they waiting for the sparrow to sing?

The spears of grass cut the rippling of water
        into haiku ravens were memorizing.

Were they teaching the stones to speak?

Cattail sprouts and watercress painted the water.

Tendrils of cottonwood roots
        waded in the river up to their knees.

Shadows of ancestral farmers
        held tight to their fence posts.

There was no place for me to dream.

I wanted to watch the buds of willows
        to open, to welcome butterflies and ants
        to their honey.

I wanted to read the haiku that grasses
        had cut from the river.

If I stepped into the river, would
        tamarisk sweeten my blood? Would
        bees swarm around my head, filling
        my eyes and ears with pollen?

Would you recognize me when I returned home,
        the spring bud of my willow-heart singing
        the love song from this May river morning
        where I was baptized in light?

14 May 2010
Santa Fe, New Mexico

Self Portrait, January 2012

> *"If you are willing to live day by day,*
> *with the consequences of love . . ."*
> —David Whyte: *"Self Portrait"*

When I write my self portrait poem,
    I will not look into any aging mirror.

I will not reread my crumpled letters
    to Mom and Dad from childhood.

Instead, I will walk my dirt road
    after a rain, look into the murky pools
    of water to read my wrinkled face.

It is woven of reflected decisions
    that fill my path with fertile adventures.

My face will be the map to home
    where I took off the mask
    when you kissed away the emptiness
    from my journey.

This is the self portrait I write
    on my ceiling with words of praise
    when I open my eyes at the morning gate
    to find your shadow lying next to me.

18 January 2012
Santa Fe, New Mexico

The Road

When I walk my road
        on ice-filled January mornings,
        I might feel the beginning of time.

There is a sound of crushing snow,
        a gasping of freezing water.

Somewhere on the road
        is a map to town,
        away from where the fruitless orchard
        lies waiting.

I see footprints of wild animals
        that carried the night away.

On tops of wooden fence posts
        are mounds of snow
        that have argued with the sun for days.
        Their debates have freed the cold,
        melting it into loaves of silence.

My road has no end.
        I have given it a beginning at my door.

When I sleep in the chill-filled night,
        it is the hunger for my morning walk
        that rests on my pillow
        before the day breaks the glass in my window.

15 January 2007
Galisteo, New Mexico

I Tell Myself How I Should Write a Poem
—for Frances Hunter, poet-friend

Clear a table.
Cover it with an inch of blank paper,
      unlined or lined, your choice.

Remember lines can be boundaries,
      so choose unlined.

Gather all the pens and pencils in the house:
      all the pens you ever had. A pencil
      sharpener would be a good thing to have.

Select your most uncomfortable chair.
      It will keep you awake. Soft pillows
      are dangerous for poets; they remind
      us of our mothers.

At sunrise, without breakfast, sit at the table,
      face a window view of the sky or the branches
      of a tree. Imagine the spaces between the
      branches are where the voices of the world
      come through to you.

Begin to write the name of who you love.
      Add the sound of weeping.

Use verbs that describe your love-making.
      Fill your page with adjectives that tell
      how your love tastes and smells.

If your tears have left wet spots on the paper,
      write into the pools of dampness. The ink
      will spread, forming a picture of who loves you.

Begin again. Write the date of your birth.
      Tell how it felt to leave your mother's womb.

Write how you bled from being beaten with silence.

Write how you laughed when the sparrows circled
    your head singing.

Write how you understood loneliness as a child
    understands loneliness.

Write what the ravens told you when they left
    feathers on your doorstep.

Write your story as if speaking to God.

2 May 2009
Santa Fe, New Mexico

This is the Land Where I Live
*—for Michael and Evangelia (Lisa) Lucas
and Aphrodite (Titi) Andreopoulou*

There is only light on the land
      where I live.

Shadows of footsteps never live
      long here.

Stones roll down the hillside, dancing
      with bright-eyed fence posts.

The trees that are here flail their branches
      into silver necklaces.

When animals cross the fields,
      the river calls them to drink
      from its lucent fingertips.

Leaves never pile up upon themselves.
      They vanish when birds sing
      as the sun sets.

This is the land where wild roses
      have no thorns and lost cows
      disappear into the willows,
      leaving a contented afterglow.

I want to leave this land as I found it,
      not an easy thing.

I watched two apple trees die,
      how they fell over without a sound,
      lay there among grass and crickets.
      They became smaller, glowed phosphorescent
      in the moonlight.

When I walk by them on warm nights,
      I speak to them. They answer
      in a soft luminous voice.

19 December 2007
Santa Fe, New Mexico

The Genie

Today is the day
        I shall meet someone.

I shall call him shadow.

I shall recognize his face
        stolen from my mirror.

His footsteps will be filled
        with rainwater.

There will be the songs
        of spring frogs.

There will be the drumming of thunder
        marauding with singing stones.

He will stand there,
        his feet just above the earth.

There are no footsteps behind him
        in the dust.

If we rub the lamps of our hands together,
        a genie will appear.

10 September 2007
Santa Fe, New Mexico
Published in Santa Fe Literary Review, 2008

Feeding the Fire

There is a fire in my kitchen
      that will eat years of asking questions,
      leaving only a pile of silent gray ashes.

There is a fire in my heart
      that flickers and flames
      at the whim of a photograph
      or a handwritten name on an envelope.

I will shovel my winter fireplace,
      drop the ashes into a glass bucket,
      layer the vanished trees
      into my garden on a windless day.

I will smear the ashes from the burning
      of my heart across a sheet of white paper
      to remember where they came from.

The burning will say it's over.
      The wound is healed.

What ashes remain, I shall spread into my garden
      with the others, where the seeds of memory
      bloom and ripen with spring plantings
      and the conversations of mourning doves.

In the Summer, when I pick the first zucchini
      and open a leaf of lettuce,
      I will taste the name of the beloved
      in the greenness of what I have left behind.

13 January 2007
Santa Fe, New Mexico

Drawing with Crayons
—for my daughter Jain Kelain

My daughter sits circling her paper
      in red and purple crayons.

Stunted arms with three fingers,
      a belly-button, two legs with dots for toes.

But I might be naming things
      that are not there.

She has put a pointed green hat
      with a purple tassel on the circle of a head,
      added eyes, a nose, a red mouth.

I can feel the pressure of her crayons
      in the silence.

If I sit quietly, I might see her again,
      looking in her box of crayons for blue
      to color her mother's eyes.

18 November 2006
Santa Fe, New Mexico
Published in Oracle, Vol. 6, 2007

Crickets

On Monday mornings, half a white sheet
      floated from the wicker basket
      onto the floor, a cloud folding over the ironing board.

The kitchen smelled of warm night visions,
      the scent of remembered travels
      between stars, the moon lying
      on my pillow, listening to crickets.

The iron moved across the sheet
      with the morning-soft palm
      of my mother.

I watched as the sheet crossed the board,
      was folded into a book for my bed.

It was Monday night. I crawled into
      my mother-scented sheet, her hand
      ironing love across my shoulders,
      softening shadows, the moon slipping
      into my bed.

The crickets.

The crickets.

8 August 2008
Santa Fe, New Mexico

12 December 2008

Such stillness under this white sky
        is the emptiness of trees,
        where leaves the color of earth
        lie calm among stones.

This is December silence: a place
        to rest without luster.

This is a colorless day:
        the transparency of faceless
        window-glass and the mist
        whispering from the river.

Everything is here only because
        the magpies have flown away
        and I have found my footsteps
        to return home.

12 December 2008
Santa Fe, New Mexico

The Spaces Between Your Name and Mine

Now I can name myself the poem
        carved in the tree-trunk.

I've been lingering in the sun
        long enough, avoiding lichens
        and moss, too vagrant to become
        a stone in the wall.

If I count the years I am without you,
        I am the tenth fence post
        at the river's edge.

I listen to the cat who sleeps near my shoulder.
        She pulls the blanket over my head.
        We purr together before counting stars.

If I call your name with the blue letters
        of the alphabet, do not run away.

I have latched the gate to the meadow
        with a loosely tied cotton rope.

The path to the spring where cattails grow
        is a short one. Your feet will not stumble.
        The stones tell magpie stories.

Listen! They will tell your fortune:
        tell you where the treasure is buried.
        They will open the spaces
        between your name and mine
        for the day to end without breaking our hearts.

19 April 2007
Santa Fe, New Mexico

Self-portrait at 80

I hold margins of sky and sea in my eyes,
        the left eye, the Aegean,
        the right eye, the sky over Okinawa.

My head is my orchard in Autumn,
        ripening apples, falling leaves,
        lichens, an erratic magpie nest
        emptying of dreams.

I keep travels about the earth
        in the map lines
        running about my face.

They lead to the open fields of my cheeks,
        where hollows lie open
        for hungry mosquitoes and kisses.

The canyons between my eyebrows
        guard the first cry of the first born,
        the embers of an early divorce,
        the pleasurable confusion of aging.

The upper lip is hedged
        by a graying moustache that appears
        to erupt from either nostril.

The Irish nose is strong enough
        to hold the flood of tiny sprouts
        back in their caves.

There is an inverted smile
        in the chipped and dented chin.

This September, the face has the blush
        of a winter morning having
        overstayed its visit.

Across the forehead are four lines,
        waiting for a poem to be inscribed.

Tonight I will look into a mirror
    after the company has left
    to tattoo the words across my brow
    that rhyme with life and death.

2 September 2008
Santa Fe, New Mexico
Published in Santa Fe Literary Review, 2009

Poem for Laura Gilpin, Photographer
—for Mary Randlett, Photographer

She was the tripod on the Camino
        and in the arroyo near Rough Rock.

She stood headless under her black cloth,
        focusing on a trail of dust
        following the Navaho sheep
        or Old Lady Tallsalt washing
        her dishes with a single cup of water.

Laura was the generosity on the Camino
        and on the mesa near San Ildefonso.

She stood headless under the black cloth,
        focusing on the light-splotched adobe walls,
        where shadows of dancers were a frieze
        of undulating, whispering mystery
        or pausing between strokes of her shutter
        to share fry bread and hot coffee.

She was the camera-eye of a goddess.

She gave vision to those who would greet her
        with her glass-eyed lens that mirrored
        the warmth of her garden flowers opening
        in the snow when the leaves of her
        cottonwoods had fallen to mulch.

She has left behind the gifts of her
        black and white memories in books,
        on the walls of hogans, adobe houses,
        museums and on the underside of clouds.

I only need to look up into a winter-filled
        sky to see her—cloud woman—focusing
        on the earth, where she danced
        under her black cloth.

15 January 2009
Santa Fe, New Mexico

A Cup of Tea with Paulette
—in memory of Paulette Beall

It was the dove in her that I visited.

The way she poured the amber line of tea
        into a cup, the curve of her wrist,
        a weed sprouting.

How she passed the cup of tea to where I sat,
        giving the most sacred gift of the moment.

How she spoke of the light passing
        through ripening grapes,
        speaking of them as a cluster of earth's eyes.

How her words wove sentences and fragments
        of her breath into a blooming garden
        of colored daydreams.

How her fingers moved when she held her teacup,
        playing her cup like a harp,
        giving the air around us currents
        of lemon-scented air.

How she listened to me, weaving my words
        into something so important
        the flowers on the table became brighter.

It was as if we were sitting on an altar,
        two people who became burning beeswax,
        and the room filled with the incense of our being.

It was the dove in her that I visited.

And when I am most quiet, the world around me
        empty of itself, she comes to pour my tea
        into the soft feathered cup that is the moment
        I am most empty.

6 August 2006
Santa Fe, New Mexico

The Portrait of Uncle Nap

I draw a portrait
    I have never drawn before.

I shall use a soft hair-brush
    to whisper,
    to speak like water.

I shall use brown ink,
    not only the color of his eyes,
    but the color of the earth
    he breathed in each morning.

I shall draw the portrait
    on a weathered board
    from the family barn
    on the North Fork of the Newaukum.

The board is from the river-side
    of the barn. Stains of floodwater
    have left streaks of white,
    the whiteness of his hair in moonlight.

If I begin his portrait
    on a warm afternoon in August,
    I will sprinkle the pollen of sunflowers
    on the paper. This is where the sun burns
    an image of his tenderness.

I have no need to complete this portrait.

He died too soon.

21 August 2007
Santa Fe, New Mexico

Listening to Childhood Drawings

Who was to know
        that these crayon drawings
        in grade school were to become echoes
        into the future?

The dog that walked to school with me,
        licking my face, waiting
        for the piece of bread
        from my paper lunch bag.

The squeak of swings in the playground,
        where I could fly beyond
        the airplanes if I closed my eyes.

There is the drawing of the car,
        big windows for watching rain
        on the highway when I sat alone
        in the back seat.

Sparks and splinters to scatter about
        in later years,
        creating the jigsaw puzzle
        with pieces missing.

I didn't know how important the fish
        I caught with my father would become
        or how important the crocheted
        potholders would be until I burned
        my fingers in my own kitchen.

I find chunks of time never come
        together except by the glue
        of memory, when there is nothing
        else to say to the fragments
        under my feet.

When I look for the crayons in the boxes
        in the closet, I want the red to flare
        into flames, the blue to fill the sky
        of the room and the white to be winter-white
        to cover the house in snow,
        where I make the footsteps
        that follow me each morning.

28 December 2007
Santa Fe, New Mexico

The Wind is Lonely

I can not wait for a full moon
        to paint your face in the mirror.

Your face was the halo in my eyes,
        the light that bleached my hair.

Your face, the sudden rain
        left on pine-needles.

Now, when the moon searches for you,
        I remain still, a statue
        that my tree weeps for
        when the wind tears the leaves away.

14 November 2008
Santa Fe, New Mexico

Breaking Camp

When I leave,
      the lake will come with me
      and the house with the loose-shingled roof
      that sang in wind storms.

The tree-line edge of the mesa will be gone.

No one will hear the water running
      over river stones as I heard them.

No one will smell the green
      of rain-tipped cedars as I smelled them.

No one will spin down my road
      after summer dustdevils as I did.

Nothing left behind was mine;
      even the snow did not keep my footsteps.

I learned early that birds sang to one another,
      not to me. I kept their songs in a basket
      of loosely woven twigs.

I learned that trees blossomed for their fruit,
      not for me. I ate pears with sunshine
      and juice running down my chin.

When I leave,
      the skin of my fingers that touched
      those I loved will disappear.

I will take away an orchard and a sky
      and the voice of magpies, leaving
      for you the silence
      to fill with your footsteps.

I will take laughter and tears with me,
      abandoning the night
      for you to fill with roving stars.

I leave behind my poems
        that hint at how my heart burst
      from too much blood.

14 December 2007
Santa Fe, New Mexico

The Soft Edge of a Mountain

I want her to butterfly my night
      with hands that tie a rainbow
      around my neck, squeezing my breath
      into the voice of a river.

I want her to pile the stones
      in the darkness into a stairway
      of words that spell the future.

Now as the wind blows clouds
      into the shape of her portrait,
      I can lie on my back in the winter grass
      to see her eyes close for the last time.

I can watch her vanish once again,
      leaving only a cloudless sky
      and the soft edge of a mountain.

4 June 2008
Santa Fe, New Mexico

DRAGONS

*The astonishments of poetry, for me,
reside most vividly in its capacity
to make a reader receive utterable
and unutterable realities at once.*
—Jorie Graham
*American Women Poets
in the Twenty-first Century*, 2002

*I find myself increasingly impatient
of any kind of writing, prose or poetry,
which does not bring with it the coiled
energy, the dark tincture of the unconscious.*
—Nuala Ni Dhomhnaill
The Irish Times
16 May 1992

Time of the Dragon

There was a time
    I bared my belly to the dragon,
    all prickly, vulnerable,
    mother-of-pearl bright.

You were there.
    You soothed the hackles of scales,
    shining the words toward dawn
    by opening your eyes.

Caution lay on the cobblestones,
    gray mutterings where I stopped
    before the entrance to the cave .

No virgins remained, only words
    inscribed on the walls:
    Welcome Angels.

There was a time
    the signs came down.
    They were indecipherable
    in their own language.

Claws inverted, worn away by moonlight
    and love songs, I yearned for
    a familiar duet.

I can not tell you more.
    Dragons dwell on mountain tops
    in caves lined with a soft-petalled fresco.

It is the pain of reawakening
    that stutters and shakes the stones loose.

Your eyes remain unblinking.

                20 June 2007
              Santa Fe, New Mexico

Fragments

I will keep you in my night sketches
        away from the children
        and the cats sleeping in the kitchen.

It is because you come so often,
        apologizing to the emptiness,
        that I know your face.

You are there alone, sometimes on your knees,
        more often standing, legs apart, red-faced,
        mouth not moving, hands clenched,
        holding secrets you could never share.

The long nights are your safe places,
        your dark caves with loose stones
        for crushing skulls.

There are enough white pebbles nearby
        for spelling HELP on the mountainside.

The last time you asked forgiveness,
        you left your glass eyes on the bed-stand,
        telling me you were born blind.

                                    2 January 2010
                                  Santa Fe, New Mexico

The Missing Parts

I forgot to clean the windows.

The dust blows in with the memory
    that darkens the glass,
        leaving patterns to be read like tea leaves.

It is difficult to keep the wet fog of you
    from crawling under the doors,
        surrendering stains on the walls.

I have said welcome again and again,
    thinking it was you knocking,
        you writing your name in the dust.

Such is the description of a broken heart.

You had no words of warning in your eyes.

You had no words of warning in the heat
    of your hands.

There are few choices in emptiness.

There is nothing to ask for when everything
    is nestled among gold nuggets.

When do we learn about land mines,
    except when holes are blasted in darkness?

I was willing to lose my feet.

                        2 January 2010
                      Santa Fe, New Mexico

The Departure of William Witherup

Bill has left us.

When a poet dies, the earth is silent
        for a brief time.

Trees hold their leaves in stillness.
        Stones press a little deeper.

Clouds change their shapes.
        They rest against mountains.

Only the wind breathes
        not to speak for him
        but to exhale his words again
        in the deep silence
        where he blessed us
        with his songs of praise
        while cursing pollution and cell phones.

Bill has left us
        with time in our hands,
        with his love and fury
        and gentleness in our hearts.

Bill has left us his bow and arrows.

He entreats us to keep the bonfires blazing.

for remembering
10 June 2009
Santa Fe, New Mexico
Published as broadside
by Nancy Dahl, Blue Earth Press, 2009

Stealing Time

I remember the glow of red cherries
        in the oilcloth at breakfast.
        They gave juice to the awakening daydreams.

No one sat too long at the round table.
        There was something waiting
        to carry away the bread crumbs
        and the after-taste of warm milk.

The trail to the playground was paved
        in hopscotch squares of sidewalk.
        Five squares for Monday through Friday.
        One square for the ants that crawled
        from noon to darkness.

I would stop to speak to the morning postman.
        He would show me the stamps on letters
        from foreign countries. I could spell
        Switzerland and Rhodesia.

Today I can see the dust from the felt erasers
        clouding the classroom where I sat
        adding a page to the geography book
        showing where I lived between the
        South Tacoma swamp and the 56th Street
        hill where crows described
        what night hid from me.

18 May 2007
Santa Fe, New Mexico

The Homeless Man

He left the city,
>carrying holes of childhood in his pockets.

His fingers looped through his belt.

He walked just above the earth,
>leaving no footprints.

The roadway rustled autumn.

Crickets emerged from under stones,
>singing when he passed.

His face, a neon of loneliness,
>his hair tangled with moths,
>eyes the leaves from a book
>of endangered birds.

I saw his arms holding emptiness,
>bruised blue.

His back straight, where bees
>had built a winter hive.

The sound of wind rushed
>through the harp of his ribs.

Statues on the cathedral watched
>his shadow pass by, waved their wings,
>tears running down their stone cheeks.

>*23 October 2008*
>*Santa Fe, New Mexico*

The Sound of an Echo

No one can explain the night
      to dogs and widows.

What is lost becomes a menagerie
      of bones and wedding rings.

On the path up the hill
      stones open their wings
      to let dragons slip by.

Songs are etched on broken eggshells,
      hiding in abandoned nests of robins.

Somewhere dawn rises in fields of raspberries
      that magpies press, preening their feathers.

If I call her name from across the lake,
      waves appear in the shape of lips.

Nothing has a softer kiss than the foam
      at the edge of water.

Perhaps the breathing of turtles
      is the sound of an echo.

Perhaps it is in the opening of hands
      we see the words given to us
      by our mother before we were born.

Nothing is heard when the moon
      vanishes over the mountain in the West.

If I live long enough,
      I will give my skin to a coyote.

6 July 2007
Santa Fe, New Mexico

GUNS   GUNS   GUNS

They broke down our door.

They never knocked.

They yelled words we never heard before.

They never knocked.

They wore metal helmets and carried guns.

They never knocked.

They rushed into the room.

They broke our jar of drinking water.

They tore open our cushions and pillows.

They screamed   GUNS GUNS GUNS.

They never knocked.

They tore the curtains to the room
     where our children were crying.

They never knocked.

They tore blankets from our children's beds.

They screamed   GUNS GUNS GUNS.

They tore clothes from my husband,
     made him naked.

They screamed   GUNS GUNS GUNS.

They tore up our rugs.

They pulled our grandmother's picture from the wall.

They screamed GUNS GUNS GUNS.

They never left.

They never left.

They never left.

30 July 2009
Hotevilla, Arizona

MUST SELL HOME: Call 986-6066

Dad died just before Christmas. No Insurance.

I sold the car and most household goods
        for some St. Vincent Hospital bills.

Mom died with heart-break on New Years Eve.
        Not much to sell for the funeral.

We buried Mom in the orchard under her favorite
        apple tree, the one that always bloomed first.

Wells Fargo foreclosed January 8th. Manager said
        we had nothing they could get their money by
        selling and we had six days to leave.

The grand kids wanted the old family portraits.
        I took them out of the frames, sold the frames
        at the indoor flea market for forty dollars

Rose quit the community college, got a job at
        Walmart, gets $9.50 an hour. She's sleeping
        in her car somewhere behind Village Inn.

Carlos has an extra room at his place in Las Cruces.
        I can have Rose drive me down on the weekend.

The real estate people come by every day now.
        They say they are lowering the price again.
        It was built of adobe by great grandfather
        Tafoya in 1880.

Orlinda, the astrologer, says my bad luck
        comes because I have four sixes
        in my telephone number.

6 January 2011
Santa Fe, New Mexico
Published in Malpais Review, Autumn 2011

The Loneliness of Ashes

Ashes from last night's fire
        lie silent as dust on the window sill.

She lights the fire with a single match.

Flames nibble the arms of dry wood.

A warmth touches her cheeks,
        paints her face into a winter rose.

Nearby is the sound of horses galloping.

They pass her window without sharing
        their frost-covered body heat.

Their silver-stained breath joins
        the fog whispering in the valley.

Their ears are twitching pendants,
        celebrating the solstice morning sun.

Once she searched in the prairie
        of their eyes, where summer grasses
        were dancing.

She had to turn away before butterflies
        blinded her.

Now as the fire begins to warm the kettle,
        she follows their long tails sweeping
        snow from winter willows where rabbits
        are hiding.

She turns, pours water into a cup
        of wild herbs she gathered in September.

She will drink to the one she loves,
        burning her tongue with the words
        he gave her when he left for war.

Ashes from her fire will greet
    her in the morning.

She will find his fingerprints
    in the dust on the window sill.

25 November 2008
Santa Fe, New Mexico

My Winter Soldier

My brother played drums in his high school band.

He sang Bacharach songs to Fatima down the road.

He tickled my mother with a peacock feather.

He laughed at my 4th grade elephant jokes.

He teased Dad about his bright ties.

My brother came home last week from Iraq.

He wore a piece of shrapnel from his shoulder
    on a chain around his neck.

He had a prosthetic arm with five plastic fingers
    in a white glove.

He called Dad a motherfucker because he wore
    a tie.

He said he had shot elephants and peacocks
    in the Baghdad zoo for target practice
    with his buddies.

He said Fatima was just another stupid Hajji.

He sold his drums on e-bay.

Last night at dinner he told us how they poured
    gasoline on a library in Fallujah, shooting
    into the shadows until they ran red.

How the books burned; even Rumi couldn't escape
    the flames.

He cried in his room all night, tossed grenades
    of four-letter words into the dark.

This morning he never came down to breakfast.

18 March 2008
Santa Fe, New Mexico
Published in Against Agamemnon: War Poetry, 2009
Published in Sin Fronteras: Writers Without Borders, 2009

The Edge

Let me tell you about the edge.

To know the edge
        is to live at its brow, at the border,
        a horizon on one side,
        a chasm on the other side.

No beginning and no end,
        except when I stutter.

To live on the edge
        is to be possessed in darkness
        with a single keyhole of light
        for breathing. Here is where
        walls are looking for color.

There is sharpness here,
        the sharpness of gasping for air,
        for taking in bird feathers,
        broken trees, the scent of cedar.

And dullness, the dullness of jumping
        into a valley of fog
        that wild animals have abandoned.

This is where I stomp on the grapes of blindness.

This is the lonely place.
        I come here to be alone,
        leaving my shadow behind,
        nailed on a fence post.

This is the place where a poet destroys words
        to find new meanings for darkness and light,
        the place where feelings are sandstorms
        and typhoons, where I take off my shirt
        from too much sweating, a place where
        I taste my salt.

It is the trap I never abandon
>	so I can find my way home.

This is where I find it most easy
>	to love and to be loved in the hollowness.

There is no map, no signboard.

The edge has no name when it is discovered.

It's like digging a ditch with a spoon
>	to bury the rainbow. What is left
>	is the sharp pain of something
>	lost I never had.

This is the place I cut open my chest
>	to give my heart to what loves me.

23 October 2009
Santa Fe, New Mexico

The King at the Corner of Agua Fria and Guadalupe

I have been given over eighty years.

Fatima was killed at twelve. Her memory
        lies in shattered glass.

I have been given the good health of my grandfather.

Ruth died at fifty-four, her lungs burned to ashes.

I have been given a home to provide me peace.

Months ago, Silva in Sri Lanka stopped looking
        for the family's table and three chairs.

I have been given two gentle daughters.

In Gaza, Hassan has made a tent with his wife's
        embroidered tablecloth for his two daughters.
        It rests against the East wall of the mosque.

I have been given freedom to move about the earth.

Kate dances in her hand-propelled wheelchair.
        She has no legs.

I have been given friends to cherish
        and words for poems.

José stands in the cold at the corner of Agua Fria
        and Guadalupe. He smiles at me driving by.

My blood turns to wine.

4 January 2009
For Three Kings Day
Santa Fe, New Mexico

Claws of a Lion

There were carved oak legs on a table
        in the hallway, knobby as my father's knees.

The feet of those legs ended in the four paws
        of a lion.

At five, I puzzled at those lion's feet,
        claws holding a crystal ball
        that lay flat on the hardwood floor.

When the adults came to play their games of cards
        in the living room, I crawled under
        that lion-footed table to trace the claws
        and the ankles of those legs.

I heard the gnawing of the chisel carving those feet,
        the laughter of hunters with guns.

I felt the softness of the fur between my toes.

When I put my head to the floor
        I could hear the lion stalking through grass
        where a small animal hides,
        trembling with fear and loneliness.

23 December 2006
Galisteo, New Mexico

Shadows with Names

I searched for the birdness in my father.

He may have been born with feathers,
      but I saw him only in blue coveralls
      and heavy black work shoes.

On cold mornings, he would warm up
      the truck before driving away to work.

He left a dark oily puddle on the garage floor.

When the noon sun came through the window,
      the oil bloomed into iridescent pools of color.

In second grade when we shared family stories,
      I could describe my father's truck,
      give its license number and the amount of air
      in each of the four tires.

I could describe how to replace a burned-out
      headlight and how the front leather seats
      smelled of wet dog fur.

Now that Winter has arrived along the road
      into the city, I watch how trucks have no
      ghosts of exhaust following them,
      how there is no rumbling scars of sound
      from brakes.

I want to see cracked windshields and to feel
      the jolt of bumpy roads.

I want to stretch out my feet in the front seat
      of an old truck to push crumpled maps
      and single cotton gloves under the seat.

I want to rub my fingers across the dashboard,
    where dust has gathered in the cracks
    between knobs of a radio and the stem of a choke.

I want to close my eyes to smell the loss
    of childhood among boxes of apples
    and sacks of cement.

But all this has driven away, leaving skid-marks
    left by heavy black work shoes.

17 November 2009
Galisteo, New Mexico

With Light on Water
—for my daughter Jeni Keleen

Let me write for you
        a poem of light on water,
        each word written from the long heavy breath
        of quicksilver,
        each word falling into
        the open window of night.

If you will,
        take my poem from this unlined page,
        set it lightly under your tongue.

I want the words to flavor any sadness
        that lies on your pillow.

If I could,
        I would write you a poem
        that hovers backstage
        when your shoes are empty,
        when the seeds you planted
        do not sprout.

You and I need poems that vibrate
        as light on water,
        that when they leave us,
        we know the ringing in our ears
        is the voice that calls us back
        to the beginning
        where it all began
        and we are listening to one another
        for the first time.

                                        2 July 2005
                                  Galisteo, New Mexico

Fishing With Brass Spinners

I had a fisherman father.

He had a son who drew pictures
        and wrote poetry.

I had a fisherman father
        who kept his fishing pole
        next to the kitchen door,
        his woven creel clean,
        his fishnet untangled,
        his brass spinners polished
        to catch the sun-stroked waters.

He had a son who thought fishing
        was for grown-up men
        who liked baseball games.

It was a calm weekend in Astoria
        on the Columbia River.
        The fish were not biting.

My fisherman father and Uncle John
        had pulled in their lines
        that spattered water about the boat deck.

        "It is time to go in.
        Pull your line into the boat."

The brass spinner on my line
        wagged across the bow of the boat.
        A salmon snagged it.
        I held tight.

Oh! Such instructions!
        "Let the line out!"
        "Keep the line tight."
        "Play the pole!"
        "Let it drag!"
        "Tighten it up!"

"Let me have the pole!"

"No! I'll do it."

It was a struggle.

The fisherman father called:
    "Keep the line coming in!"
    "Let it out!"
    "Bring it in!"

That salmon knew the kid needed him.

He came to the boat's edge.

The uncle dipped the net,
    caught the fish,
    brought it on deck.

The salmon smacked back and forth

Lay still.

The boy and the fish eyed one another

6 February 2006
Santa Fe, New Mexico

There are Hoodlums Inside Me

There are hoodlums inside me:
        shiny black leather jackets
        with silver studs, tight jeans,
        buckled boots, a hair style
        that would put Elvis to shame.

They emerge at unexpected times and places,
        burning bushes, sending flames
        in the shape of snowflakes and dirigibles
        over rooftops into Heaven,
        such fires enough to make God blush.
        Even Jacob's ladder couldn't reach them.

These hoodlums have good hearts.
        They sing and dance in dark alleys,
        chase dogs and rabbits,
        steal apples and newspapers.

I welcome my hoodlums. They spice up my journey.

18 December 2008
Santa Fe, New Mexico

Ask Me for Bread and Water

*One must try everything
to recover memory, it has
so many hiding places.*
—Lawrence Durrell in *Clea*

They come in the wind, arms outstretched,
      pressing their bodies into my passport.
      I stumble, stuttering names.

The one called marriage is tarnished from tears,
      crumbs of shiny brass
      peering through the clogged keyholes.

The one called youth springs onto my shoulder,
      rips holes in my shirt, throws buttons
      into the garden, pinches ears,
      fills my shoes with sand.

Another, the rigid uncle, who tripped me
      into a bedroom of rose-filled wallpaper
      with thorns, has turned to dust.

And another, who walks beside me
      on the dusty road edged in barbed wire,
      snaps his suspenders and tells stories
      learned from crows.

Others pass by, waving their wands of fire
      and ice, erasing lines on the map
      where I traveled and paused, waiting
      for them to catch up.

When I push the stone from the cave,
      where memories are painted on the walls,
      I find my brushes filled
      with everlasting colors.

Now I will look into the pool of memories
        to etch a hotspur face on the mask
        I thought I had lost.

If you see me on the way to the market,
        ask me for bread and water. I have enough
        to last until we get home.

4 June 2008
Santa Fe, New Mexico

The Last Icon

I am at the end of my life.

Paints are drying up:
>the blue of Panteli Bay,
>the salad green of basil,
>the diva red of Ephagalia's summer umbrella,
>fig purple,
>asphodel white,
>the yellow of Leros Island lemons,
>the cat orange of Michael's sunsets.

I want to leave something anonymously
>to be discovered
>by a beachcomber.

I have gathered rounded Xerokampos stones
>that nest into the palm of my hand;
>one stone fits glove-like, warm,
>belongs there, begging for my paint.

Here, I chose one holding mica moons.

And the image to paint:
>a vision of days to come,
>beyond saints and dragons,
>beyond the view
>of an earthly paradise.
>I've done all that.

My fingers are scarred from the scales of dragons
>and their firedrake breath.

I want to paint the dream I had—the one that comes
>just before dawn—the gift with no cross,
>no blood, no wailing women, the dream of a light-filled
>room with a single mirror. Where there should be a floor,
>there is the sea reflecting the sky over Patmos and Leros,
>gently ebbing in and out, covering a mosaic,
>my hand open, outstretched.

2 September 2010
Santa Fe, New Mexico

ABOUT THE COVER ART
Acknowledgment to Mr. Evangelopoulos

Dragons have been part of my fantasy life from Asia through Greece. Stones have been part of my waking life from being a collector of agates, a geology major in college, gathering rocks in travels about the world and from my creative life as a sculptor. On the Greek island of Patmos, these came together in St. George and the Dragon painted on a stone!

Patmos is noted for the Monastery of St. George the Divine—founded in 1099 by St. Christodoulos—and a living community of traditional icon painters.

Long-time Athens' friends, Michael and Ephagalia (Lisa) Lucas answered my query about this icon painted on a smooth island stone, which I purchased many years ago on Patmos:

"The original ikon from which this painting derives is probably hundreds of years old, painted by some monks in a monastery. Over the centuries, this ikon has been copied repeatedly to decorate a modern orthodox church or simply to sell to tourists, notably on the Plaka area, for which there is a flourishing industry."

So I thank you, Mr. Evangelopoulos, for your inspiration for *Valentines and Forgeries, Mirrors and Dragons.*

—James McGrath

ABOUT THE ARTIST

Catherine Ferguson is a poet and painter living in Galisteo, New Mexico. Since 1973, she has been painting *retablos*, a New Mexican tradition. Inspired by landscape, animals and trees, she creates watercolors, oils and poems that express her love for nature. Catherine teaches *retablo* and watercolor painting. She is the author of eight chapbooks. In 2007, she received the New Mexico Book Award in Poetry for the book, *The Sound a Raven Makes*, a collection with two other authors, Sawnie Morris and Michelle Holland. Catherine enjoys writing with her friend James McGrath, sharing the surprises and the joy of life.

ABOUT THE POET

James McGrath is a wanderer about the Earth, frequently straying about Greece, Ireland, Japan and other mythically-related lands in search of Valentines, Forgeries, Mirrors and Dragons. James is a poet, artist and teacher. He lives in an old adobe house in the traditional village of La Cieneguilla, Santa Fe, New Mexico. He is known for his narrative poetry in the KAET/PBS American Indian Artist Series of the 1970s: *Charles Loloma, Allan Houser, R.C. Gorman, Helen Hardin, Lonewolf and Morning Flower*, and *Fritz Scholder*. His poems have been published in nineteen anthologies. His collections of poetry, *At the Edgelessness of Light, Speaking with Magpies* and *Dreaming Invisible Voices*, are published by Sunstone Press.

James was creative writing instructor at the Institute of American Indian Arts in Santa Fe in the early 1960s. He spent twenty years teaching and as Arts and Humanities Coordinator for the Department of Defense Overseas Schools in Europe and the Far East.

He was Poet-artist in Residence with the US Information Service, Arts America, in Yemen, the Kingdom of Saudi Arabia, and the Republic of Congo in the 1990s.

James regularly attends the Listowel Writers' Week in Listowel, Ireland, and has worked with Natalie Goldberg, Joan Logghe, Sharon Olds, David Whyte, Mark Doty, Marjorie Agosin, Alastair Reid, Nuala Ni Dhomhnaill and Eilis Ni Dhuibhne.

www.ingramcontent.com/pod-product-compliance
Lightning Source LLC
Chambersburg PA
CBHW031138090426
42738CB00008B/1138